73

Dearest Anna —
Thank you for putting poetry books
in my hands all those years ago.
Full O!   xo

Ordinary Cruelty
Amber Flame

℅

Write Bloody Publishing
America's Independent Press

Los Angeles, CA
WRITEBLOODY.COM

Copyright © Write Bloody Publishing 2017
No part of this book may be used or performed without written consent from the author, if living, except for critical articles or reviews.

Flame, Amber.
1ˢᵗ edition.

Edited by Stevie Edwards
Proofread by Nona Leon, Madison Mae Parker
Cover Design by Ashley Siebels
Cover Art by Heather Hart
Interior Layout by Kayla Shelley

Type set in Bergamo from www.theleagueofmoveabletype.com

ISBN 978-1938912-70-2

Write Bloody Publishing
Los Angeles, CA

Support Independent Presses
writebloody.com

To contact the author, send an email to writebloody@gmail.com

MADE IN THE USA

Ordinary Cruelty

ORDINARY CRUELTY

it was my mom who gave us all the words.

WHERE I WENT WHILE YOU WERE DYING

this poem is

*(about when your mother
collapses in front of you)*

the emergency plan you don't have
when the emergency

comes.

not knowing your mother's or sister's or sister's
blood type.
medications.
history.

is

*(about your mother
telling you she is
dying and then _____)*

in lieu of health insurance.
anxiety over social worker called
height weight charts. or

is

*(what your mother's
face looked like
without oxygen)*

the story of your mother
saving your newborn life. or
waiting to find out if you've returned the favor.

this poem

*(is about prying your
mother's teeth apart)*

wonders whether you did all you could.
says it will let you know.

this poem is

*(this is not a poem.
about her saying
she was dying)*

hope that grinds you down.
neither here nor there.
cannot remain present.
not a gift.
will not firm no or yes.
passes hours without blinking its eyes.
without waking up.
does not know how to leave.
a horrible bedside manner.
cold hands and bad breath.

this poem is   *(this is not a poem. about*
                                                      her pitching into your arms
                                                      and _____)

the stuff your mother is made of.
nothing you recognize.
what's under skin deep.

THIS POEM IS A

yo mama joke. is trying again
to be funny. this poem is all yo mama is so
dead. your mother is dead. this poem can't be
funny. sweats onstage under the lights. this
poem is awkward pauses where the audience
was supposed to _____. the audience didn't
_____. the audience throws rotten
hearts onstage. boo
hoos.

this poem is a joke. not haha so funny
or roll your eyes. this joke (that is also a poem)
is like quit playing. that's not funny.

this joke has gone on for too long. is
interrupting your birthday. is 36 days past
its point and this better be fucking
hysterical. this poem is not hysterical.

is not weeping and wailing. is slow seep
from a wound that will kill you (better get
that looked at/oops too late). this poem
is dead already. cannot believe it.

did not disintegrate. this
poem whooshed up in flames. burned hot.
left you its ash. this poem is not a joke. is
a not funny quit playing. this poem cannot find
its end. punch. line.

HOW I KILLED HER
after Anastacia Renee

1.
once you pried and pried and pried until the lid went pop and out
came all the paper snakes except they weren't paper and there was no
shaky laugh just the shakes. and the snakes hissed and slithered all over
the rooms and slithered their way into the twists of your hair and out
the lids of your eyes tiny wagging curling tails.

*my mother tells me there isn't much to say. her voice is like why are you
bothering me with talking about him but her eyes shift like these answers
are important for you but i don't want to say. i ask questions that are less
obvious, come at it roundabout. she wants to talk. she says that is always the
problem, she wanted to talk, she was their friend, she was never trying to get a
boyfriend. what about him i ask and she says she didn't know him very well.
and her lips press shut. there isn't much to say.*

2.
once you poked and poked and poked until the scar split into fresh
wound but the puss stank and the infected flesh was still there inflamed
and swollen. and you knew the tainted blood had already reached your
heart and it was maybe inevitable that instead of killing you it would
only make you poisonous.

*i don't understand why you didn't abort us. my mother flinches and then
says she tried. once. she flinches again and amends to say she succeeded once.
what did my father look like? i think this question will be easier but she is all
twitch today. you, she says. you. i watch her track my glass to my lips again
and again. i do not ask if i act like him. there isn't a happy memory in the
bunch. brown eyes and quick smile. our dead almost babies and foolish hearts
and whose story is whose.*

3.
once you pulled and pulled and pulled until the door burst open and
the bones came tumbling out disintegrating into ash as you coughed
and spluttered and choked. and the tears that poured down your cheeks
mixed delicate bone china mask you drew over the telling tint of your
flexible skin. all give and compromise.

my mother says my name like she is a worn out dishrag. like all bacteria and ew. this is the voice that tells me to stop. tells me don't go there. i am remorseless in my need. to know. how i came to be. just like her. him. and so my ?&?&?& hooks into her skin and i peel back slowly as if it will sting her less and she gives like liquid. i stand ankle deep as the water rises and her mouth is a sewer flooding and there is no happy ending just waste.

RESURRECTION, OR *UNRESOLVED* *ABANDONMENT ISSUES WHEN YOUR MOTHER DIES*

tell the one where she   comes back

just to leave you again, tell
the one where she was not   gone

anymore tell the one where she
is here again by magic
tell the one where she is   crunch crunch crunching
shovel scrape tell the one where she
is back
by DNA reconstruction, from a piece
of you,
amber, tell the one where she is sand
    castle you build from ashes

tell the one where she was not ever gone, tell that one again and again
and believe it. tell
the one where she

turns blue then grey then collapses
tell the one where she turns blue then grey then collapses
telltheonewheresheturnsbluethengreythencollapses tell the one
where

she is back by human sacrifice tell the one where she

blames you and is not wrong   but
is still gone, tell the one where she

comes back just to leave you again

IN THIS INCARNATION

your mother is cashmere

you open your chest where you keep her

find a flock of moths released

each bellyful a small gift

SEE NOW

how everything
is crooked. jokes hang
skewed on the walls and
good news is burnt
on the bottom. smiles have
wrenched their knees out
and each conversation a
stinging hangnail. sleep
stumbles down the last
few stairs and joy
is sodden drunk in the corner
where sour stomach smile
gathers dog hair dust bunnies.
malcontent, an ever-present sun,
so even the nightmares gather
sweat on upper lip.

MY GUILT COMPLEX AS INHERITANCE

you have decided you will be the best
and so you:
make playdoh cupcakes and
rollerskate and
read Winnie the Pooh with voices and
paint and
watch movies eating Popsicles and
she falls asleep in your arms
sticky fingers and cling and
all you remember is how she said
you broke something – a promise
to take her swimming today.

ORDINARY CRUELTY: SUCKLE

when your nipple slips
from her glutted mouth
you fall asleep dreaming of her
churning your joints into milk
you dream of flight with these
newly hollowed bones and lips
wrapped round them like straws
how gladly you make meal of yourself
for her consumption; a feast
you will call love. as if animals could
refrain from feeding when hungry.

EVELIA (AT BEDTIME)

she is fresh bath
skin and soft cocoa butter
sweet she is also
i don't want to go to bed
she is petulant whiny
i'm not tired and
i wish i could stay awake
forever and
mommy just going to
the bathroom! and do you
have something to eat I'm
still hungry and
i wish i was a grown-up

and two stories
and a song
and a hug and kiss
and a high five
and an i love you
and i'm a sucker because
bedtime comes
thirty minutes later
all the time

she will be sleepy high-pitched
hello mommys and
i love you so much and
aw that's sooooo adoooorable
kisses and tickling and
snuggling and sluggish
mornings
but just now, i catch
her last
slow blink
to sleep

like a blessing,
lightly, between
my eyelashes
her hand is warm heavy
in the hair on
the back of my head
a blessing

THE DAILY GRIND

you are powdered sugar
ground
no place to sit or lay
ground
you are toddler no tiara
ground
mortal and pestle
ground
you done met a
hard place, a rock
and a soft spot and
still ain't no place to lay
your head
and it won't hide you
neither, nor hair
you are ground down
ground around
profound ground
and you figure that
with the hole it's wearing in you
you gotta be wearing a hole in it
and you wonder if when
you get that hole if
you'll be too ground down
to see it through

BOY, AGE 7

my seven-year-old nephew wants a gun

wants to be an army or navy or air force guy
does not want to learn to read.

"let's be knights"
he says to his brother,
"we will guard
the princess"
meaning
the girl.
meaning,
he will wield the sword.

he loves to dance but
not when anyone is watching
:"boys don't dance"
he says
he wants to be like the man
who makes his mother cry.

BODY LONG ENOUGH TO FILL THE TUB,

my naked child delights in her bath
her limbs an easy tree-thing growing
she has been built along curving
lines; a heft.
          don't I look like a woman
No.
she pouts at this answer, wants
at least a little bit: she is six. woman
is
          I bet I look sexy
No.
before knowing what sex is: cannot
reach it soon enough.
I debate when to tell her of
inevitable blossoming and bursting
her own skin thin and scarred, ritual
murder scene between thighs cyclic
she has already been red flagged.
hushed warning of what becomes
of beautiful brown girls, how
fascination can peel them open.
ripe fruit split -- the juice;
how they all want to squeeze.

IN WHICH YOUR DAUGHTER MAKES FRIENDS
WITH THE NEIGHBOR BOYS

and suggests truth or dare but
when dared to kiss the one boy
pecks him on the shoulder
"real quick" and is "that
is gross" innocent limbed and

does not see how the older boy
puts words in the mouth of the younger
how he is ain't no fun if the homies
can't have none gonna get himself
a kiss and your daughter is just six

stands sway back belly forward
one knee cocked and just wants her
turn so she can say something gross
to do like bugs or butts

but has been too beautiful meaning
"are you prepared to lock her up/
you are gonna need to watch out"
from the moment she learned to smile

and it's today, right now, for the first time
you ever want to really do this;
think of thick walls and locking doors

you can see how she's enough
to be a mouthful and they
are already drooling.

UPON RETURNING FROM A FOREIGN LAND, OR SITUATION NORMAL ALL FUCKED UP, OR ANOTHER DAY BLACK IN AMERICA

i've been home for
      24 hours
                  one week
          6 days or
ten minutes;

i am sitting in LAX waiting for my flight.

i have not been home for
      3 weeks
eight hours
                over a month
      4 days or

i am still not home; always going
        (one of these things is not like the others)

        about to leave,
i do not live (anyw)here.

i am in mourning for _____
how i lost my
      home/way/will
how i left my
      hope/child/choice

how (there is blood mixing with the lotion)
    my daughter's voice lost to siren wail
how (i cannot get the gunsmoke from her hair)
    fear and defiance dance (gas and bullets competing
    for her skin)

i am not silent, just choking on _____
how there is no over before the starting again, how
      (one of these things just doesn't belong)
there is no way (____).

WHAT TO BRING TO A DIE-IN

leave:	bring:
security blanket	bulletproof vest
inescapable skin	reliable witnesses (white)
tongue	choking throat
justification	guns

and if not your guns, then your wide screaming mouths
and if not your screaming mouths, then your gasping tears
and if not your tears, then your fist clenched in anger
and if not your fist, then your hands raised in surrender.

bring your own body
pulsing; add the heat of your children.
the ones still left living. lay down.
be empty. silent. become the ideal
image of you. don't _____.

brace for impact.
expect them to shoot.

YOUR NEPHEW GIVES YOUR DAUGHTER A TOY
GUN FOR HER BIRTHDAY

and you imagine retaliation
you imagine her riddled;
you gift her a story of dead brown skin
and the child who once inhabited it:

your nephew, pale and safe,
is worried; says the story
of the dead brown thing is scary
how the cop just _____
how the kid just _____.
your daughter agrees, refuses to play
even inside, even where she is _____.

you realize maturation means presents
come with an edge, sharp or
bitter. she's big now. it's time to watch
out for giggles ridden with gunshots.

EVELIA (BEING SICK)

she is quiet. doesn't complain. says
she feels fine, and she means it.
i am unprepared for the way her bones
rattle disagreement and her mouth opens
suddenly, effortlessly, gushing to prove
the lie. she is still quiet, now messy. says
she feels fine, and she means it. says
she could keep down chocolate and if
i will just keep my hand on her forehead
she will be all better by morning. i am
unprepared for the calm in my stomach and her
unending trust that i can make it all
right, not with chocolate but with
electrolytes, and how easy she can
rest in my arms.

GOVERNESS

when he comes roaring up on my ass, i am angry.
not like, really, really angry, just like
"whatever dude"
as i continue passing dude on my right

when he screams over to the far right exit lane
roars past several cars to cut me off   and brakes
i am angry. like, pretty angry.

like what the fuck dude but i don't say it

despite my sporty little zippy car
i am, in fact, driving 3 kids to the pool
so i can get my fat ass in the water and work out
and we are late i smoothly

roll into the left lane, to pass.   he cuts me off again

and brakes.
now i am black girl angry, like, what they would call
"unreasonably" angry
like all hell naw
and you done pushed a bitch too far this time
and all literary and shit too, like woman scorned

(don't underestimate this heifer)
                and hell hath no fury

                          and shit.

he veers off to his exit and quickly comes to a stop
i roll past, glancing to see his gloating smile

                            wave

over my child's head

i swallow rust and revenge

the music   from the radio is suddenly full
of tiny pulsings of squish and flex
    from three small hearts flush with blood

to remember i've learned when
    and how   and

where it was important to quit   playing.

CHORE CHART IN THE FORTRESS OF SOLITUDE

superhero makes time to sit down
for a meal. superhero
did not take off cape
                        until meal was prepared.

        superhero alone.
                        for the moment. gloriously.

superhero sure chaos rings out   somewhere.
                        superhero ignore it. to eat.
superhero already changed
the toilet paper roll.
emptied the garbage.

 superhero breathes after a swamping tide of mundane.

superhero knows superheroes do laundry.
how thick ice be in that fortress.
how solid the solitude.

                        superhero answers to _____.
                        if superhero tells you,
                        superhero would have to kill you.

superhero knows   how killing is a villain's work.
superhero knows   how tempting the night.
                             how unobserved.
                             how it creeps.

superhero sits down for a meal.
knows how to shoulder the load   after filling a belly.
                        and how to run empty.

AN OCTOPUS ESCAPES THE FISHING NET:
ADVICE FOR MY DAUGHTER AS CEPHALOPOD

in this life, where you must be both
predator and delicacy, rend
for yourself the tenderest bits.

enter a world, daughter
where you may drink brine and not be
pickled;

lose remorse in the hunt for that which feeds
you. be sure
there are eight passions
for each arm's embrace,
in case your dreams are injured
or cut short.

by all means, keep yourself
whole, even as you adapt with grace,

honey love. my
sinuous structure
pure musculature   and give;

infinite flex and reshaping, do not
be confined to any that would contain you.

be gentle relentless
manipulation; hang on, love,
or disappear   in the confusion of your melanin

clouding the display; how they love

to watch you squirm   and ooze;
be not object
entertainment,   remember how
to pry open exits   remember
camouflage.

learn both lurk   and listen;
eyes open to color of danger
of safety

do not forget that tucked up
in the unfurling of your
pretty petticoat   of a body:

you are thought and plot. beak
and brain. predator and delicacy.   Feed.

MY SISTER AT 40 WEEKS, OR ONE-AND-DONE FOR ME

(1.)
everyone knows you don't really want to be here. you are alien animal enough to smell the gun smoke and taste how asphalt licks blood, and you want none of it. you bulge the belly, both content and restive; try to avoid the detection of ultrasound. our impatience with you is not in your reluctance to arrive but the futility of it. the spaceship crash landed, there is no return.

(2.)
she asks me if i am done having kids. i choke and sputter on the likely ash of my daughter's bones wrapped in the burning rags of her flesh, bullet ridden or shell shocked. i have empty hands when things go awry. fear is fevered breath i keep my lips clamped down around. determined to clench helpless around my own flesh-dug nails and not make my daughter comfort object. security blanket. shield. i weigh percentages. yes, i say.

(3.)
we have done our best at cajoling you. you say you do not want words and can tug umbilical for all the other sweet things this world can possibly offer. you say look, see how big we are getting, we are just fine staying in here. no one wants to tell you that you are becoming your own kind of monster. that you are sure to rip and tear; what you might become if you begin with shredding your mother.

UPON INHERITING

your predecessor's inbox
your mother's estate
your father's fear of commitment
your country's least-valued skin

                                                                    each
                                                          a
                                        common place
                        every day
            run-of-the-mill
ordinary

cruelty.

MOMMY NEEDS A MINUTE

i do not want to be a bad mother certainly not the kind of mother who would curse out her kid when it isn't really about the kid, whose only fault is a sweet voice that hooks under the cracks in my skin and pulls and yanks and tears further i am not wanting to be all in pieces and definitely not all in pieces all over my kid, who doesn't deserve the mess and isn't old enough to understand much less go get the broom and i try breathe and count to ten and mommy needs a minute but still i do curse out my child with no real provocation excepting the prattling on and on and on and i already barely know my own mind or recognize myself these days so i can't handle *but mommy or I'm just going to or why do i have to* because i am wondering that my damn self and so i snap and lash out hating every word venomously spurting from my mouth wondering why my breath is rotten and i can no longer stand the sound of my own voice.

LITTLE GIRL BLUE

this little girl has no magic
stick left
no presto or abracadabra
this little girl forgot to believe
her wand was more than
plastic and glitter paint
that rubs off in the sweat of her palm
this little girl talks
grownup serious
about death and how that means
you can't come back
this little girl is not sure what
not coming back means
but knows she is supposed to
be sad about it
this little girl has no magic
stick left
has floated off the surface
because the wind blew strong
almost enough to blow her away
she is all a t-shirt and skirt
do not make a dress
dissatisfied
all princesses have long hair
and my hair is only long
in the bath
unhappy
this little girl talks
i wish you weren't the boss of me
but isn't adding to the list
of things she'll do when she's grown up
(curse and drink liquor)
anymore

because the grown ups have told her
it ain't nothing but work up here

at these heights

and this little girl has no magic
stick left
to see it
differently.

NE ME QUITTE PAS

i do not pretend to understand
the ways in which she is absent

or the way she lost faith in friction
or her ashes

will not purse lips
gently to breathe

instead i offer an invitation
spread her destruction

to the pulsing red of flesh
beneath my skin

trust she will not cut split burst
(w)hole.

ORDINARY CRUELTY: SUCK

when she rises shaken
from betwixt your still
quivering thighs and you want to
fall in love hoping like earthquakes
everything has shifted and
she has tongued the dark
sticky center of your being like
all the way up in your pussy and
she was something to soothe you, if not
something for you to keep; if
you cannot last at least burn. as if
animals can resist snuffling prey.

CRACKING CORDS

you'd like to sing anything
but this _____ & low- _____
blues. like to sing a praise song
to the angle your lover's neck curves
into her shoulders, slopes
rounded over collarbones:
you want to sing *hallelujah* hymn.
to the blissedblessed rhythm
that can rock you *like the rock*
of ages; you want glorious worship
to pour from your throat over
spreading thighs and *dear* _____
sighing, you want to. your voice
is harsh. raw with how you *cannot*
feel the spirit moving no
more; no transcend or levitate. no
ghost-catching the holy. just welling
moan of discontent: your _____
is gone and your _____ *is aching*
and your *blues so blue they b(lack).*

:AND THIS IS WHY SHE LEFT:

it's not for me to lay claims on silence
or women
when i have nothing to offer but
a regard that stutters out of step
won't answer the phone &
promises nothing &

who wants a love that rarely
makes the to-do list, anyway?

If You Look Out Your Left Window, You Can See the Detonation Site

I want to tell about the aftermath

Because it doesn't matter so much, what happened,
what counts are the days you walk around
like a desecrated tomb
all open-mouthed and body-absent

When you are left
sweeping up the detritus of your sacred
because the riches are gone and they've left you only a mess

I want to tell about the aftermath

the nights you come bumping back into your itching skin
only to find your arms are aching
from holding yourself together
and you have nothing, nothing to help you
through the countdown to the inevitable
eyelid droop

the nights when success means you
didn't call to ask for confirmation
that you truly are the barren wasteland
they've already chosen not to love

I want to tell about love's ugly,
when it's twisted and broken
when you are a mess

Tell about the aftermath
not about what they did, but about
how you find yourself parked outside their house in the
rain just so you can ask for them
to come back to you, this is embarrassing,

just so you can see who they've replaced
you with how they aren't better than you were before you
became this mess

how the
next day you find your car is a crime scene there is blood
on the seats and your heart is,
unfortunately
still thumping wetly against the floor mat
where you wedged it under the brake pedal

I want to tell about the mess you make of yourself for love
the little
compromises and pieces you shaved off to fit their desire
how you find them curled like dead skin
on the floor of your empty house
and you forget how to fill the space around you

I want to tell about the aftermath

cataloguing
of everything you never liked in them anyway
so you could wish
you were the strong one
you were the one to walk away

I want to tell you
how it saps your bones of the marrow
the absence of their breath in
the night is blowing lonely on the empty reeds
how, with a body this hollow,
you should be allowed flight
but you are grounded here
in your mess

and so you
sweep
sweep
sweep

:TICKTICKTICKTICK:

there is a beast in my belly who's always hungry
he's already eaten one baby, remorseless
gobbled it whole, and 3 relationships too,
like memories
you can't remember forgetting
this beast in my belly drives me feed
he digests voraciously, like *:life is short*
who has time for grief or even
the process of scarring:
the beast won't let me name my dead things, offspring, kin
:bits of flesh and the blood of the meat:
he is pleased it all made it into the compost
toilet, coffin without my assistance
just a *:sigh:*, mistaken for a belch. i didn't want them to go
but there's never anything to miss once they're gone.

SURPRISE PACKAGE THE DAY AFTER

in which the flowers you receive

for your mother's death instead of

valentine's day don't bloom and as

they yellow you want to peel

them, pry them open, force them

into petal and you fixate on wanting to

do this instead of how today all your

former lovers are coming to know

their current lovers the way you

open mouth kiss grief: biblically;

today is after all a day to make love even

to your mother's corpse with these

flowers that die stingy and pinch-lipped.

YOU DECIDE YOUR DEEPEST CUT

is shaped like your ex-lover's
new lover's pussy. you compare it
to the picture your ex-lover has
shown you of the new lover's mouth:
always wide open, always loose
-lipped fleshy. you compare it to the
picture your ex-lover doesn't show
you, thighs of the new lover spread
knees akimbo; you imagine the
new lover's lips between your
clenched teeth, how they would look
as a wound bleeding.

AND FOR THE NEXT TRICK

she pulls a long chain of paper dolls
from her cunt, dresses them
tenderly in their paper pleats, ribbons, bows
says nothing of pulpy insides,
the chopping, sawing, pressing thin
excreting thick juice and such delicate
renderings; yesterday she birthed
origami swans, four in quick succession

EVELIA (IN GLIMMERS)

it looks like love sometimes
the way i will rise for her
on demand like
i ain't got better shit to do
like the warmth of her
golden brown strong arms
is all i need in the way
of heat
it looks like i know my
boundaries, these days
how much i can flex
and give
and give
and give
and flex some more
and the expansion feels like
breath, like rib-cracking
love, like the best
embrace, she has
the best embrace
still alive
and i breathe out
made up fairy tales and
silly reworkings of songs
and i breathe in
origin stories and
corny puns
her small fingers warm
in mine, matching
hop skip jump twirl

for every stride
it looks like i know my
boundaries for warmth

on demand i will rise
and give and flex
all expansion and
rib-cracking
love

i's just a tired woman after a long day of being black.
after Anastacia Renee

i decided there is not enough oxygen for me to breathe and them too. i decided i ain't gonna be sharing my seat on the bus and the train. i stiffen my spine in that unconscious way, like white woman do her purse when walking past a young black man, i ain't fin to let just in case. i start huffing my breath quickly, getting all lightheaded with my greed and smiling i smack my lips together and hums a tune on that illicit air i be holding. i feel i is too old for you to be able to take my hardwon oxygen from me, too far away from anything that looks like love and fear, too. i ain't scared. i is lightheaded and sure i know better. now. i spread in that conscious way, like white boys do when they don't want no black girl sitting next to them, i won't make it comfortable to share my space nor my air neither. i decided there just isn't enough of it. decided your blues ain't like mine. i don't have time to explain that i ain't mad. i's just a tired woman after a long day of being black.

REQUEST FOR SERVICES

will someone come raise my child
just for a little bit
perhaps a night or two

will someone cultivate this young seedling
to bend without break
perhaps a storm or two

perhaps i shall sleep or
fuck or do laundry
& praise you as god-sent

HIGH-FUNCTIONING _____

enough of my friends hang out in
graveyards like
on a sunny day or whatever for me to have developed
romantic notions or something like
maybe a tombstone will be peaceful
— enforced peace you know cause obviously otherwise I'm
sure I'd find some way to fill it up
with an anxious review of
all the things i always have to do plus
I'd wonder if maybe I'd enjoy something else
with my free time unexpected
something better like maybe seeing
a Bruce Lee movie instead of looking at his headstone
and also I
got enough   voodoo
in me to think maybe laying up all over other people's graves is
possibly bad luck and pretty
disrespectful plus
graveyards are really just a metaphor for wanting time and
being okay without company and
i don't have any and totally am

:BECAUSE IT'S NOT LIKE YOU HAVE TIME OR ANYTHING TO MISS HER:

or really anyone
mostly you just miss sleep and nice hot fresh meals where you
neither have to cook nor clean nor pay but
you are really usually totally okay
with this whole alone business and it isn't
*   even shitty, really, because you got*
hella stuff to do and never enough time or
help or energy and should one
say you're alone truly when you have a _____-year-old who can
talk you into oblivion and plus all these thoughts
about everything and all that stuff to do plus?
i don't think so, in fact
you don't really know what leisure time means but apparently
some people take it -- meanwhile
you're on the bus trying to imagine a silence
without wondering any how
*   long til's or how do you get back to's because*
it would probably be quiet except for me and
the lack of patience you have
for silence and stillness anyway and yeah,
turns out this is pretty much how you prefer it, so:

SMELL MY VICTORY

i have no grievances tonight
can abide my own company
i am all old pajamas
and funky armpits
worked hard 8 days a week
and kept it pushin
i am we don't need no invite
to no party we are the party
tired tonight
i spent my last twenty dollars
on rum and pad thai
it is the full moon
i would enjoy company
so i throw my head back
and laugh at a marathon of *bones* on netflix
dead desiccated bodies are hilarious
i roll my eyes and pout at
the neighbor too loud upstairs again like
that bitch don't ever work sleep or shut the fuck up
i sit in my own goddamn magic circle
company unto my own self
it's alright that my friends didn't call me back
i know it's raining because i can
hear the tires outside my window
flinging growing puddles back into the air
i have done something big today
i can hold the space for
funky armpits
and full
and moon
and howl

and work tired
and alone happy
and _____
and _____
and also _____.

SMELL MY DEFEAT

lately i am working most at
forgiving the failings of the body
my body, specifically
i have to breathe deep
through the hint of a double chin
and recommit to pushups
when i notice my skin
laying wrinkled and loose
but it is the knee
that bothers me most
with it's inclination to buckle
and inability to kneel
this is a dangerous and precarious
position to take: there is
give
and pain
and submit
and pain
and a proclivity for it all.

i wonder if i could forgive
such a large failing
a hindrance
in a lover
if i'd compromise lovemaking
positions
to accommodate an ailment
a permanent injury
an acknowledged falling apart
i think this is perhaps
a large part of why

i don't date: there is
give
and pain
and commit
and pain
and an attachment to watching it all go.

PERMANENCE.

it's all been a lot of quick
goodbyes, not *oh I'll miss you*
shucks wish we knew each other better
we should hang out before
you go
it is not all feel good vibes and see ya parties no
last minute brunch on her way
permanently out of town
it's goodbye like feedback on microphone
sudden emptying of the church when
the spirit has departed
it is not we are gathered here and dearly beloveds
last page good book
it's goodbye like sudden flight of birds
quick intake of breath
a startle
while you were watching

Nothing Smells Like My Mother Anymore & I Am Starting To Forget

My nephew sniffs me, says
He loves the way I smell, I
Am anxious after shower the next day

To have him sniff me again, he
Pulls away from clean hair. Says,
I like the way you *really* smell.
Don't worry, I laugh, I'll get funky again
Tomorrow.

I wonder if, for him, it is like
Crawling into her sheets when my mother
Was not home,
But suspect it is more like

The burrowing I am driven to
When she has vowed
To never return.

When the Dog Bites, When the Bee Stings

Your favorite thing has become making your ex-lovers your closest friends. (Heartbreak.) The way you can then keep them close to chew your heart in memory. Your favorite thing is how they gnaw without knowing. How you let them. How your belly gluts full and unsatisfied. (Hungry.)

WHEN IT WAS MY TURN, OR, WE CAN'T BOTH BE BROKEN AT ONCE

years later, long after injury
        original
had been forgotten

                        your cum hardened shards
it wasn't so bad,
the cut and rip

        i didn't know it would hurt me so
taking all that broken inside of me

                        the way my heart
                        pissed blood

                pushing way
            through my skin
here in the hard crust heel of my left foot
there the soft tissue give inside my left bicep
                and here in the expressive thumb of my
                right hand

            the way each catches and
shreds

NOTHING TO SEE HERE, OR MOMS DON'T HAVE SEX

when i decide to write about sex like i want it again, i am pulled back into my 13 year old self. to ricky and joanna. the "it" couple. the field trip to skateland where my mad skills whipping me around each curve were no substitute for the lowdown belly fire i felt when i watched them place their bodies together. (voyeur)

when i decide to write about sex like i want it again, my child will not fall asleep in the bed beside me. i myself could drop to sleep within five minutes. there is no groove. no squirm. no heartsqueeze shuddering through chest head rush. my blood is not rushing. (static)

when i decide to write about sex like i want it again, i start with looking back and then around. to the absence. the lack. the fear that i will want it only to not have a chance again, and what it would take to put my body in parts up for offering. (exhibition)

UNINTENDED CELIBACY, OR WHEN THE VIBRATOR AIN'T ENOUGH

i.
times like this i am sure i know how the wildfires get started
wonder what kind of grandeur there is in being the first ember
that ignites california
this year.

ii.
i sometimes assume an innocence,
pretend wonder at what goes on
in the no-mind of blowing flame

how a touch is so much more than a touch
if you know exactly what must follow.

iii.
I try not to think about dropped match
sudden ignite
how it crackles and
smokes.

iv.
on particularly hot days when
the AC isn't working and we are all
guard against anything causing
friction, i think: i do not want

the burn. sheen and blister, no,
only the way it makes my skin flush and rosy,
flirtation before it can crack;
peel.

v.
tomorrow i will not touch anything
i will not open my mouth; this is not
the desert,

too much here is consumable,
desiccation a risky

want.

YOU WILL FIND IT

whether you actively seek it or not
tucked like a forgotten 20 dollar bill in the pocket
of a purse you don't really use but that once.
or maybe more like lint pushed deep against the seams
as if the tips of your fingers were trying to press it into
the wholeness of the cloth.
you will find it like one more serving
of the only meal you crave
left wrapped neatly and ready for reheating.
there will be no reason not to partake,
not to claim it for your own.
and you will, you will state affirmatively
possessively:
say, "this is my hope."
definitive. and then it will fly
away again.

HUMMINGBIRD
after L Lamar Wilson

                                              like a

                         wail   the water
                                              moan
wade   child   mmm
       time   layer
i   child
       inhale   shout
way   trouble   time
       in   the water   gonna
                                  as i
as   i   moan   sometimes

   in   wade
                    die   a long
i wanna   layer
                                  wade   shed
       keep   rise

              motherless   from   home
                                  keep

when   i   feel
                                            salvation
                    wade   in the
motherless   gonna

              trouble   die   easy

when   i

    wail   mmm   easy

water   wade

shout   home   trouble
                 salvation
     keep   layer
god   keep
          in   the water
     easy   i
             rise

ACKNOWLEDGEMENTS

for the humans who made me what i am. i owe these words to my
mother, my sisters, my chosen ones.

& my daughter, without whom i am not god.

gretta
margo
mandy
terry
evelia
roma
renee

Original drawing in Cover Art used with permission from artist Heather Hart.

The following poems have appeared in previous publications:

THEThe Poetry, *Infoxicated Corner, 2016 Spotlight Series*:
- where I went while you were dying
- an octopus escapes the fishing net: in which my daughter becomes cephalopod
- your nephew gives your daughter a toy gun for her birthday

Winter Tangerine Review, *Hands Up Don't Shoot: Exploring what it means to be black in America*
- boy, age 7

Nailed Magazine: *Poetry Suite*
- upon inheriting

Redivider Journal
- chore chart and the fortress of solitude

wicked alice
- what to bring to a die-in

Black Heart Magazine
- "my sister at 40 weeks, or one-and-done for me" published as "40 Weeks"

Hysteria Anthology
- "bodied long enough to fill the tub"

intelli-pop: *The Slam Poetry of Amber Flame*
- "If You Look Out Your Left Window, You Can See the Detonation Site" published as "Aftermath"

An award-winning writer, composer and performer, AMBER FLAME is also a professional singer, Hedgebrook alum, and member of The Watering Hole tribe. FLAME'S original work has been published and recorded in diverse arenas, including *Def Jam Poetry*, *Winter Tangerine*, *The Dialogist*, *Split This Rock*, *Black Heart Magazine*, *Sundress Publications*, *Redivider Journal* and more. A Jack Straw Writer and recipient of the CityArtist grant from Seattle's Office of Arts and Cultural Affairs, AMBER FLAME'S first full-length collection, *Ordinary Cruelty*, debuted Spring 2017 with *Write Bloody Press*. FLAME works with a Black independent media company, This Week in Blackness, co-produces the Oakland Slam and teaches workshops for all ages. AMBER FLAME is one magic trick away from growing her unicorn horn.

www.theamberflame.com

IF YOU LIKE AMBER FLAME,
AMBER FLAME LIKES...

Said the Manic to the Muse
Jeananne Verlee

Write About an Empty Birdcage
Elaina Ellis

Bring Down the Chandeliers
Tara Hardy

This Way to the Sugar
Hieu Minh Nguyen

The Heart of a Comet
Pages Matam

Write Bloody Publishing distributes and promotes great books of fiction, poetry and art every year. We are an independent press dedicated to quality literature and book design, with an office in Los Angeles, CA.

Our employees are authors and artists so we call ourselves a family. Our design team comes from all over America: modern painters, photographers and rock album designers create book covers we're proud to be judged by.

We publish and promote 8-12 tour-savvy authors per year. We are grass-roots, D.I.Y., bootstrap believers. Pull up a good book and join the family. Support independent authors, artists and presses.

Want to know more about Write Bloody books, authors and events?
Join our maling list at

www.writebloody.com

WRITE BLOODY BOOKS

CPSIA information can be obtained
at www.ICGtesting.com
Printed in the USA
BVHW030628260220
573365BV00001B/1